PRAISE FOR *PILOT VISION* and JOHN MICHAEL MAGNESS

"Whether you're flying to the Moon or doing business on Earth, you need *Pilot Vision.*"
—Dr. Buzz Aldrin
Astronaut on Gemini 12 and Apollo 11, moonwalker
Colonel, U.S. Air Force (retired)
CEO of Starcraft Enterprises

"If you love aviation like I do, the flying analogies in *Pilot Vision* are a pure delight. But you don't have to be a pilot to appreciate the philosophy of my late father, Conrad Hilton, and the other business principles referenced by John Michael Magness. He charts a course for personal success in the pages of *Pilot Vision.*"
—Barron Hilton
Chairman of Hilton Hotels Corporation

"A thrill ride of a book that helps us reach for the stars! *Pilot Vision* combines wit, wonderful stories, and a lot of good commonsense ideas that make reading it both enjoyable and thought-provoking."
—Frank Borman
Apollo astronaut
Chairman of the Board, Database Technologies Inc.
Former chairman and CEO, Eastern Airlines

more

"Everyone in business on Earth can benefit from reading *Pilot Vision*. I *really* enjoyed the book."
—Wally Schirra
Astronaut on Mercury 8, Gemini 6 and Apollo 7

"Many aviators have recognized the similarity between the procedures they use to fly safely and the techniques successful leaders use to pilot their enterprises. Now, John Magness has used his easy style and personal cockpit experiences to relate these observations to our ground based friends."
—T.K. Mattingly
Rear Admiral, U.S. Navy (retired)
NASA astronaut
Aerospace executive

"For this fast-paced world, *Pilot Vision* offers a far reaching flight plan adaptable to any profession—a flight plan that, if fueled by desire and determination, can get you where you have only dreamed of going."
—Dick Rutan
Pilot of Voyager, the first nonstop, nonrefueling flight around the world

"John Magness's approach to leadership and success will work equally well for leaders of big and small companies alike. I encourage you to strap into the cockpit and hold on!"
—John West
CEO, System One Technical, Inc.

"This book forces you to answer some tough questions about how you are 'piloting' your business. In fact, you *must* be able to answer them in order to fly high in today's competitive marketplace. I commend John Michael Magness for providing us nonpilots an opportunity to benefit from *Pilot Vision*."

—Tom Hopkins
Master sales trainer
Author of *How to Master the Art of Selling* and *Selling for Dummies*™

"The pace of business today demands a fresh approach to leadership. *Pilot Vision* takes the wonder and excitement of aviation and applies it to a rapidly changing corporate world. Once you read *Pilot Vision*, you'll never look at your company or team the same again."

—Ross Perot, Jr.
Chairman, Hillwood Development Corporation
Former Air Force pilot
First person to pilot a helicopter around the world

"The metaphors and quotes contained in this book are valuable to us all—whether we fly or just dream about it."

—Twyman Towery
Author of *The Wisdom of Wolves: Principles for Creating Personal Success & Professional Triumphs*

more

"Whether you are just starting up the organizational ladder or just need a boost somewhere along the way, this book provides valuable insights for anyone who wants to be successful. Clear, concise, highly readable! John Magness is right on target."
—J.P. Hoar
General (retired)
President of J.P. Hoar and Associates

"In *Pilot Vision* John Michael Magness provides a clear, concise, and exciting analogy for business leadership. His insight will prove invaluable to those seeking to meet the number one challenge in business today: providing effective leadership in a rapidly changing environment. Read *Pilot Vision* and see for yourself."
—George A. Thornton, III
Real estate developer
Executive Vice President, Rhodes Furniture

"Just as a plane flies directly from one location to another, *Pilot Vision* gets the reader right to the point: how to be a better leader. John Magness has pulled together a wealth of inspirational instances, resources and analogies to keep the reader focused and motivated. The book is a pleasure to read."
—Harriet Briscoe Harral, Ph.D.
Principal, The Harral Group
Executive Director, Leadership Fort Worth

"John Magness offers his readers a unique insight into the common characteristics of good pilots and good business leaders. Magness reminds us that really good pilots stay focused and committed. Their relentless preparation combined with confidence and courage sets them apart. Good business leaders are the same. Anyone faced with today's business challenges will find several things in this book to add to their "preflight checklist."

—T. Allan McArtor
Former combat pilot and member of U.S. Air Force Thunderbirds precision-flying squadron
Former head of the Federal Aviation Administration
CEO and founder of Legend Airlines

Pilot Vision

John Michael Magness

Adams-Hall Publishing
Los Angeles

Adams-Hall Publishing, PO Box 491002
Los Angeles, CA 90049-1002

Library of Congress Cataloging-in-Publication Data

Magness, John Michael
Pilot Vision and other pilot secrets to succeed
in the business world
p. cm.
ISBN 0-944708-50-1 (cloth)
1. Leadership. 2. Success in business. I. Title
HD57.7.M343 1998
658.4'092--dc21 98-27851
CIP

Adams-Hall books are available at special, quantity discounts for bulk purchases for sales promotions, premiums, fund-raising or educational use. For details, contact: Special Sales Director, Adams-Hall Publishing, PO Box 491002, Los Angeles, CA 90049-1002
AdamsHallP@aol.com or 1/800-888-4452 or 310/826-1851

Printed and manufactured in the United States of America
20 19 18 17 16 15 14 13 12 11 10 9 8 7 6 5 4 3 2 1

This book is dedicated to
my loving wife and "copilot," Angie.

God richly blessed me
by bringing you into my life.
I love you.

Contents

Acknowledgments

So often in our world, we are lured by the seduction of instant gratification—microwave dinners, the lottery and crash diets. As a pilot, I have learned that all things worth having take much longer. You can't cram to become a good pilot or leader. It takes years of practice and then you just begin to learn and tap your potential. As writers know, there are no shortcuts in writing either. It takes years of research, experience, editing and rewriting. This book is a result of my leadership experience as a pilot, an international businessman and a professional speaker. There were no shortcuts.

If I have learned one thing as a pilot and leader, it is that no one ever does it alone. I would run out of space trying to thank everyone who has had an impact on my life—but let me give it a shot.

First, let me thank the many men and women with whom I have worked. I have had the privilege of working alongside some of our nation's finest soldiers, business leaders and pilots. The lessons I share with you in this book are certainly a collaboration. Just as the aircraft is incapable of flying without critical components, this book would have been impossible without these people. Specifically, I would like to thank Greg Stone, Robert J.H. Anderson, James Steele, Don Olson, Herb Rodriguez and Wayne Downing for their inspiring examples. I would also like to thank the two best instructor pilots the military ever produced, Dan Jollotta and Cliff Wolcott, who taught me that you can never be satisfied with yesterday's performance.

I would also like to thank those who provided the much needed words of encouragement during this effort: Tom Hopkins of Tom Hopkins International and Ross Perot, Jr. I am also grateful to my friends at Adams-Hall, especially Don and Susan Silver for their faith and attention to this manuscript.

Last, I would like to thank my late grandmothers and my father and mother who instilled in me an inner compass for right and wrong. I appreciate my wife Angela for her love and for tolerating my late night typing and research over the years and the relocations across the globe. And to my loving children, Chelsea and John Michael, who continue to inspire me, one day you will understand the extent of my love for you.

Introduction

Few occupations conjure more of a romantic, exciting image than that of a pilot. Hollywood and history have assured that. Consider Charles Lindbergh, who first flew solo across the Atlantic; Amelia Earhart, the first woman who flew solo across the Atlantic; the distinguished fliers of the 1940s Women's Auxiliary Air Corps who made significant contributions to the World War II effort on the homefront; the Tuskegee Airmen proving an ignorant populace wrong and with style and courage; Chuck Yeager, who flew faster than anyone thought possible when he broke the sound barrier; Neil Armstrong for taking the first steps on the surface of the moon; and Astronaut Sally Ride as the first American woman to orbit the Earth.

Whether we recall stories of military or civilian pilots, airplane or helicopter pilots, there is something about pilots that captures the imagination of us all. Maybe it is their ability to "slip the surly bonds of earth" as written in Magee's famous poem "High Flight." (See page 4 for the entire poem.) Perhaps it is their ability to operate complex machinery with apparent ease that transfixes us. We may even think how lucky they are to have been born with such a natural ability.

Nothing could be further from the truth. Over the past fifteen years, I have had the opportunity to meet, interview and study some of this country's best and brightest leaders in business, government, sports and our communities. I have looked at these people from a decidedly different perspective—through the eyes of a pilot.

What has been interesting to discover is that these leaders consistently reached new heights while exhibiting the attributes of a pilot.

During this time, I have served as a helicopter pilot and commander for the U.S. Military, a staffing consultant, an aviation consultant to a foreign government and now as an international businessman. Throughout my multiple careers, one question has driven my own relentless pursuit of success: what makes someone successful in the business world? This book was written to answer that question.

How this book can help you

You have taken a necessary first step. By reading this book, you have chosen to "take to the skies" and rise above others with daring, skill and confidence, just like a pilot. You will learn to fly above the competition. Where you are going, it is less crowded, the air is better and the view is absolutely breathtaking!

Pilot Vision invites you, the business reader, to look at the world through a pilot's eyes—to think, plan and act with the daring and the discipline, with the confidence and the precision of a highly-trained pilot.

This book shares seven secrets of successful pilots that you can adopt to become a "Pilot-Leader" in business. Starting with "Pilot Vision," the unique, three-dimensional perspective that sets all Pilot-Leaders apart, you'll see how Pilot-Leaders succeed and you will be inspired to fly higher in the world of business.

High Flight

Oh, I have slipped the surly bonds of earth
And danced the skies on laughter-silvered wings;
Sunward I've climbed, and joined the tumbling
    mirth
Of sun-split clouds and done a hundred things
You have not dreamed of—wheeled and soared and
    swung
High in the sunlit silence.
Hov'ring there, I've chased the shouting wind along,
    and flung
My eager craft through footless halls of air.
Up, up the long, delirious burning blue,
I've topped the windswept heights with easy grace
Where never lark, or even eagle flew.
And, while with silent, lifting mind I've trod
The high untrespassed sanctity of space,
Put out my hand, and touched the face of God.

—Pilot Officer John Gillespie Magee, Jr., No. 412 Squadron, RCAF

John Gillespie Magee, Jr. was an American/British fighter pilot who flew with the Royal Canadian Air Force in Britain during World War II. "High Flight" was written on the back of a letter to his parents. He wrote, "I am enclosing a verse I wrote the other day. It started at 30,000 feet and was finished soon after I landed." Magee died at the age of 19, on December 11, 1941.

1
The Making of a Pilot-Leader

"Leaders are made,
not born."
Warren Bennis

"Pilot-Leaders are made,
not born."
John Michael Magness

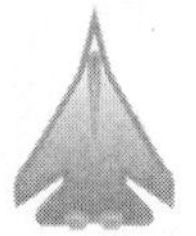 1

The Making of a Pilot-Leader

At a recent entrepreneurial conference held at the Massachusetts Institute of Technology (MIT), one common interest emerged as the attendees settled in and introduced themselves. Many of the successful business owners shared a similar non-business-related interest: piloting.

A large percentage of those attending the conference not only were licensed pilots or were former military pilots, but also owned their own plane. Why would this elite group of business leaders be interested in, even passionate about, flying?

Do pilots and successful leaders share common traits? Yes! And I'll let you in on another secret: most tend to run their companies like they pilot their aircraft.

What do these Pilot-Leaders and champions of the skies know? What insight do pilots gain with a knowledge of flying and being a captain in the air that helps them succeed on the ground?

While test flying a potential aircraft for a client, I began to see striking parallels between the flying I was doing and these burning questions. The key is to see what we can learn from the skills and acumen of a highly-trained pilot that transfers into success in the business world. Let's begin by examining the process of becoming a pilot.

The making of a pilot

We have much to learn from the making of a pilot. Many of the same attributes that a pilot develops and later hones are required for success in our information intensive, turbo-charged world.

Each pilot develops aviation skills with much hard work and a lengthy training program. Okay, genetics may play a part in one attribute—good eyes. But even without the mythological pilot eyesight, many exceptional pilots have flown with Coke-bottle-thick glasses. I have also known people who had 20/10

vision but failed flight aptitude tests. So I maintain that genetics plays only a small part in the making of a pilot.

Where does the rest of pilot skill come from? It starts with flight training. Let's look at the rigorous training of a helicopter pilot, which I can address from firsthand experience.

Every morning at Fort Rucker, a large Army post about 150 miles southwest of Atlanta, 300 helicopters take to the sky around the sleepy southern town of Enterprise, Alabama. Here, the finest military helicopter pilots learn the tools of a unique trade.

Every day for nine months, students study flight procedures, maps and aircraft in pursuit of earning the title "Army Aviator" and the chance to wear the coveted silver wings. The instructors at Fort Rucker must be doing something right. The U.S. Air Force, Navy and Marine Corps and numerous U.S. foreign allies send their best and brightest candidates to this pilot training center. The pilot training at Fort Rucker stands as a living testament that pilots are made, not born.

A real change of life

When a person walks into the U.S. Army's helicopter flight school (or any flight training program), regardless of the role he or she occupied in society before, that person walks out a pilot.

From the day flight training begins, a change takes place: the trainee begins to think of himself or herself as an aviator. The transformation is nothing short of a physical and mental metamorphosis. I have witnessed it countless times and I am still amazed at it each time. How can a new pilot help it? For nine months the new pilot eats, drinks, breathes and studies like a pilot. By only associating with pilots and being totally immersed in the culture, the remains of the new pilot's former self are checked at the flight gate.

Flying represents the ultimate learning potential of human beings. If people can learn to fly, they can learn anything. Certainly, they can learn to soar and to succeed in business. This book will show you the path to become a "Pilot-Leader," a person who leads with the same kind of extraordinary skills a pilot possesses.

The Pilot-Leader analogy

In *Pilot Vision*, I use the analogy of the Pilot-Leader as a touchstone for developing your skills for success in the business world. In this analogy, a business leader is the pilot; the leader's team is the crew, ground support staff and suppliers; the customers are the passengers; and the business is the aircraft, which doesn't run or "fly" by itself but is dependent upon the Pilot-Leader, team and customers.

You don't have to know how to fly to reap the rewards of being a Pilot-Leader—just share the burning desire to pilot your team, customers and business to new heights and certain success.

"In Summitatem Nisus" —strive for the top

This Latin phrase has been the Magness family motto for more than 100 years. It's also a great motto for any person in a business or an organization who wants to be a Pilot-Leader and fly high with their team and customers.

Your competition operates in two dimensions seeking linear solutions. As a Pilot-Leader, you will dis-

cover a third dimension of thought and creativity. Just as a pilot thinks and flies over and around obstacles, you can, too. A Pilot-Leader has the ability to use skills to move the team in three dimensions. A Pilot-Leader leads with the confidence, skill, audacity and foresight of a well-trained pilot. The world is hungry for this type of leader.

The Seven Pilot-Leader Secrets

The seven Pilot-Leader secrets resulted from my years of experience as a successful pilot and leader. I have flown and studied with some of the best pilots in the world. These aviators manage their cockpit like a chief executive officer in business. They understand and continually apply these seven Pilot-Leader secrets:

1. Pilot Vision
2. Situational Awareness
3. The Power in Planning
4. Soaring with Technology
5. Communicating Your Vision
6. The Power of Knowledge
7. Flying with Trust

Today's most successful business, sports, civic and political leaders demonstrate expertise in many of these areas and pilot their organizations to stratospheric success.

We'll look at each key area in detail in the upcoming chapters and see the remarkable similarities between successful pilots and successful leaders.

You can apply these secrets to your role in business. Then, you, too, will begin to think, act and lead like a captain of the airways.

Pilot-Leader empowering questions

Do you stand in awe of high-profile leaders and attribute their success to luck?

Are you willing to put in the time and effort to learn to lead?

Have you made a commitment to yourself and your team to soar above the crowd?

How can using the Pilot-Leader analogy give you an added edge in business?

Which of the Seven Pilot-Leader Secrets rings a bell or piques your curiosity?

2
Pilot Vision

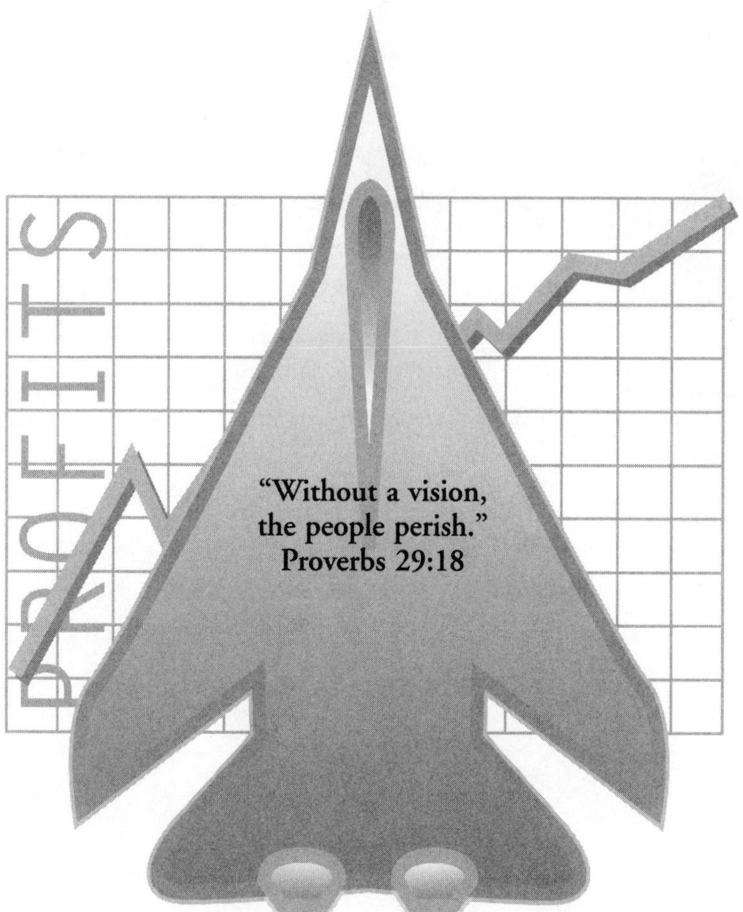

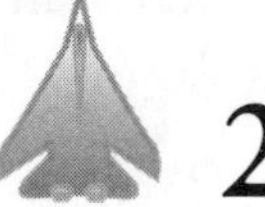 2

Pilot Vision

If there has been one problem of piloting that has been re-engineered more often than any other, it is how to enhance a pilot's vision.

Pilots have been hungry to extend their vision from the first time they took to the skies. The first "pilots" during the American Civil War flew in balloons with telescopes hoping to spot enemy encampments. During World War II, pilots had radar installed on their aircraft that could detect the enemy beyond visual range. Now, modern day helicopters are equipped with electronic optics that help pilots peer through smoke, haze and the darkness of the modern battlefield. All of these technological advances have enabled commercial as well as military pilots to see what is beyond their immediate field of view.

For a pilot, there is a distinct difference between sight and vision. Good pilots may have 20/20 or

better eyesight, but the best pilots have extended that sight to 360-degree vision and are capable of seeing and anticipating what is over the horizon. In other words, they see not only what is happening in front of them, but what is going to happen to the aircraft, crew, passengers, weather and terrain. In short, they anticipate and therefore control all influences on their flying environment. They realize that failing to control one's environment relinquishes control of the flight to chance or bad luck; hence they know that if they don't control their destiny, something else will.

Pilot Vision in business

Great business leaders also have this same vision. Having learned to control their environment, they have honed this insight into an almost surreal ability to predict and control future events for the market, team, company, product or customer. Warren Bennis, author of the book *Leaders* and one of this country's foremost authorities on leadership, remarks that "the single defining quality of a leader is his capacity to create and realize a vision."

Michael Crichton, best-selling author of *Jurassic Park*, *Congo*, *Airframe* and many other blockbuster

novels, has the unique ability to write about topics before they become front-page news. His visionary writing and marketing has allowed him to become one of America's most successful authors. Think about it: before the dinosaur craze hit our kids, he wrote *Jurassic Park*. Before Eboli and AIDS infected our consciousness, he wrote *The Andromeda Strain*. He has vision to know what will be important to his audience not just today, but in the future.

Often we stand in awe of high-profile business leaders such as Microsoft's Bill Gates or GE's Jack Welch and their seemingly divine business acumen. Rest assured, their ability is a learned trait. It is vision. As a pilot has learned to expand eyesight to vision, you, too, can learn to develop your Pilot Vision.

Improving your Pilot Vision

Helicopter pilots enjoy a unique perspective on the world. Flying at low altitudes, pilots are able to see both the details of the ground and immediate terrain below as well as what is ahead. This is where we, as leaders, need to position ourselves as well: not flying so low that we lose the "big picture" and not so high that we lose touch with our current situation. Yes, it

is a delicate space in which to operate, but it is also the optimal location to best use Pilot Vision.

Remember, pilots use their vision to control what enters their flight environment. As a Pilot-Leader, you can use vision to control the operating environment through which you lead your team. A vision is not a mission statement and not a set of goals, although missions and goals flow from vision. For a Pilot-Leader to have vision, there must be a capability to visualize what is desired for both the leader and the team. Vision is a combination of belief, experience and hard work. Without vision, a pilot stays on the ground. Without a vision, a leader yields the skies to others.

Staying ahead of the aircraft

For pilots it is important to position themselves mentally ahead of the aircraft, anticipating obstacles and providing solutions before a problem occurs. If a pilot gets behind the aircraft, the aircraft begins to dictate the pilot's response instead of the other way around. The only way to prevent this is to stay ahead of the aircraft.

Pilot-Leaders must stay ahead of their "aircraft" (their business) as well. Today's fast-paced market and ever-approaching deadlines require that you position yourself ahead and rise above the day-to-day challenges and have a future vision. When circumstances begin to dictate your every move and you no longer feel "in control," you have just fallen behind the "aircraft" and may find yourself hanging onto the tail. Warning: you are in for one heck of a ride!

As a Pilot-Leader, learn from pilots who use their vision to stay ahead of the aircraft. Their eyes are constantly moving from the horizon to gauges, to the checklist, to a map and to the terrain immediately in front of them. They are always thinking of what is going to happen next, yet they are astutely aware of the current situation. They position themselves mentally ahead of the aircraft.

British Field Marshall Bernard Montgomery said, "A good leader must dominate the events which encompass him; once events get the better of him he will lose the confidence of his men and when that happens he ceases to be of value as a leader." He recognized the need for leaders who could stay ahead and

"dominate" events, not be overwhelmed by them.

Ross Perot, Jr. has excelled both as a pilot and as a business leader. Ross was the first to fly a helicopter around the world. In a recent discussion with Ross, I asked him about the relevance of Pilot Vision. Without hesitation he commented, "I lead my companies, like I fly my aircraft." Asked to elaborate, he continued:

> "The number one rule for the pilot in any aircraft emergency is to fly the aircraft. Regardless of all the lights, bells and whistles that are going on around you, as the pilot, you must fly the aircraft first, then deal with the emergency. Too often in business we get caught up in placing blame, establishing committees and dealing with the crisis of the moment. As the leader of my company, I must remember to continue to fly the aircraft. The 'crisis' will come, go and be replaced by others; time has proven that. But if I stop leading the company and divert my attention for too long, well, we won't have a company to fly for too long, will we?"

These are words by which to live and lead.

The competition

As a Pilot-Leader, you also need to see inside your competition. This means anticipating problems, forecasting needs and taking action long before the point when the competition forces you to act—by then it is too late.

Intel's Andy Grove continues to stay ahead of the computer chip industry. By strictly adhering to Intel founder Gordon Moore's prophetic prediction that chip power doubles every 12 months, Intel strategically positions resources ahead of demand. (Incidentally, for some unexplained reason, most people think "Moore's Law" says chip power doubles every 18 months; Gordon Moore himself has refuted this common misunderstanding.)

Contrast that with the normal way of playing "catch-up" to consumer demand that many businesses follow. By virtually creating the demand, Grove and company stay ahead of the consumer and thus the competition.

Know your competition better than they know you. Successful military strategists spend years studying the strategies of their enemy. They are then able to accurately predict how the opposition will react to every action and stimuli on the battlefield. With that type of information, you can stay ahead in the business world. But remember, your competition may be trying to do the same with you.

Pilot-Leader empowering questions

In your work, where are you looking? Are you focused on short-term results or on long-term growth?

Do you routinely find yourself moving fast but not getting anywhere? Are you "behind" in the decision loop?

Do current crises preclude you from conducting future planning or market analysis?

Can you see through the "fog" of the marketplace and detect issues before they impact your business?

What information do you require to stay ahead of the competition? How do you plan on acquiring it?

3

Situational Awareness

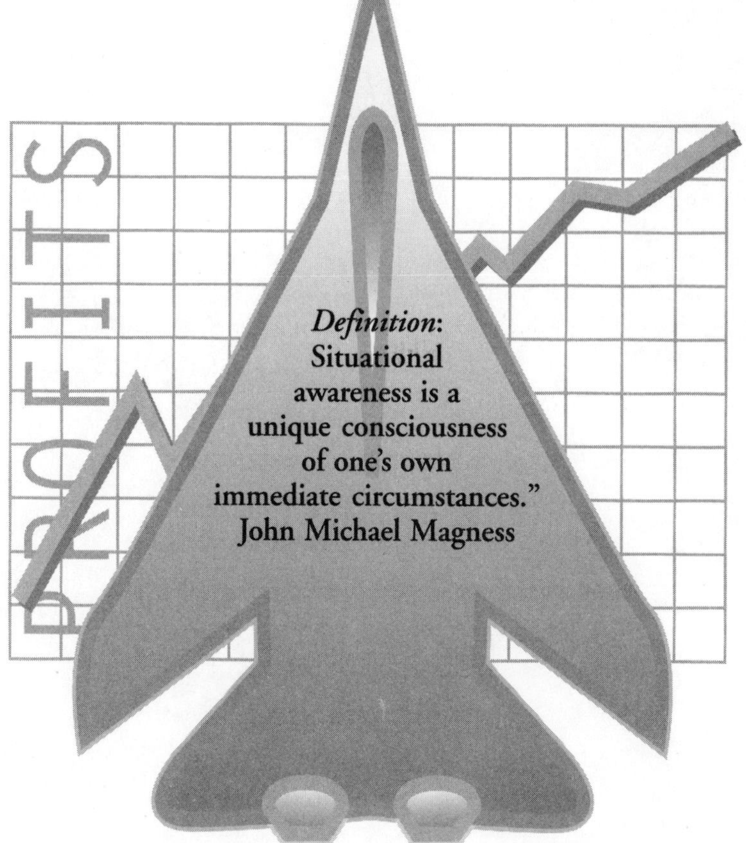

3 Situational Awareness

Some leaders have it. Some leaders definitely don't. What is situational awareness? I define it as being keenly aware of one's own immediate circumstances. Situational awareness flows from Pilot Vision.

How do you know who has it? A leader who can tell you without reference the names of all his or her team members' spouses, has it. A leader who can tell you without reference, the status of each account, project and even next problem (if any) definitely has it. A leader who can sense and anticipate the personal problems of teammates has situational awareness.

This is more than rote memorization. It is a practiced ability to make sense of one's environment and know which direction is up. Throw tough projects at Pilot-Leaders with situational awareness and they will be able to tell you not only what is wrong, but where or how to find a solution. Pilot-Leaders may

be moving in that direction already!

A pilot with situational awareness can immediately tell you the status of every system on the aircraft without looking and can feel the subtle differences if anything is awry. Over time, the best pilots learn to fly by the seat of their pants. Such a pilot trusts gut instincts and acts on them without question. For a pilot, this intuitive skill develops from many hours of flight time; a leader develops intuition from business experience, including exposure to situations requiring intuition. There are no shortcuts.

Learning to fly in the air and in business

Well before you develop situational awareness, you need to start with the basics of flight training. You'll soon see how learning to fly is analogous to learning to maneuver in the business world. So, here is a short course on flying—a helicopter, of course! Climb in, strap in and hold on!

Three-dimensional controls

There are three main helicopter controls: the cyclic, the collective and the pedals.

The Cyclic. Unlike most airplanes which have a yoke for steering, a helicopter uses a stick that sits between the pilot's legs. This stick, called the cyclic, provides maneuverability and stability for the entire aircraft.

Linked directly to the large helicopter rotor atop the aircraft, the cyclic allows a pilot's right hand to make the helicopter quickly maneuver up, down, forward and backwards or to keep the aircraft stable at a hover.

In business, you also must have this ability to move your team in different directions and be able to maneuver to avoid obstacles, pitfalls and storms that often affect your business on a daily basis. You must have a cyclic in your business cockpit. Like our helicopter, connections to your team should be simple and direct. Unnecessary layers of personnel or procedures can both delay your inputs and lessen their impact. With the turbulent business market today, you need quick reactions to conditions for immediate results.

The Collective. While the cyclic provides a helicopter pilot with directional control, the second control,

the collective, gives vertical control.

If you want to fly higher, pull up on the collective with your left hand. Want to return to the ground under control? Slowly lower the same stick. Like the cyclic, by a system of rods and levers, a pilot's inputs directly affect the whirling rotor overhead. But unlike the cyclic, the collective is also linked to the engine. As more power is needed, a pilot pulls on the collective. To fly slower, a pilot pushes down on the collective. It sounds simple and after a few flights actions become automatic.

Without a collective, a helicopter would be a two-dimensional, one-speed aircraft. The collective adds that third dimension and is the direct link to the heart of the aircraft, the engine.

As a Pilot-Leader, what provides your ability to maneuver in three dimensions? Many of your competitors operate in only two dimensions. They see problems and obstacles in the marketplace in two-dimensions and their solutions invariably reflect this. Add a third dimension of thinking and acting more broadly with situational awareness, and you will fly

right past them.

The Pedals. The third control, the pedals, lie at a pilot's feet. The pedals control the tail rotor located some 20-30 feet behind the helicopter pilot on the tail boom. The tail rotor provides directional control while at a hover and actually counteracts the rotational force of the main rotor. Without it, the fuselage would spin helplessly beneath the rotor blades. Try guiding your team or helicopter while spinning around at 200 rpm!

The tail rotor also helps align the aircraft with the prevailing winds in forward flight. It improves the efficiency of the aircraft; it allows a pilot to stop fighting the force of the wind so that the wind passes over and around the aircraft smoothly.

As a Pilot-Leader, have you ever had to change the entire direction of your team or company on a dime? Hopefully not everyday, but even so, are you able to execute a rapid shift without re-engineering your company? It is imperative that those controls (your pedals) are easily within reach and that you know how and when to use them. Are you facing a radical

parent company restructuring? It's time for a pedal input and a rapid change to the right. Maintain your momentum, but shift your focus to the right and move your team in the new direction. Before you know it, you will pick up speed and be right back on course.

What about aligning with the prevailing winds? Sometimes it doesn't pay to fight the market or even our higher-ups. By pushing on the appropriate pedal, you can align the aircraft with the winds and make your rotor system more efficient. That's using the conditions to your advantage. While other leaders or businesses complain about market conditions or external forces, Pilot-Leaders use them to their advantage and fly even stronger and higher.

Putting it all together. Now you should be getting the feel for the controls—the cyclic for direction and obstacle avoidance; the collective for power and height control; and the pedals for direction and wind alignment. As a pilot, you need to be prepared to make inputs to any or all of these to be successful in flight.

As a business leader, establish your own controls and be prepared to make changes in this, the dynamic and turbulent market of the 21st century.

Gauges

As if dealing with these three controls simultaneously weren't enough, a pilot must also be aware of the cockpit's plethora of gauges—dials, indicators and buttons. It's not as bad as it seems! Those gauges actually simplify a pilot's job and allow for safer flying.

Let's take a closer look. The primary gauges in a helicopter that a pilot requires are:

1. Compass
2. Torque meter
3. Slip indicator
4. Attitude indicator

Compass. Directly in front of a pilot lies an instrument that shows all the points of the compass around in a circle. At the top of the compass is the direction the aircraft is pointing. At the bottom is the direction the aircraft just came from. This essen-

tial gauge will be one that we will always come back to not only when the weather gets rough, but when we need some reassurance that we are headed in the right direction.

There are times when you, the Pilot-Leader, will become confused, disoriented and incapable of determining the direction you were supposed to be heading. The compass will always tell you your current heading and whether you need to steer right or left to intercept your original course. Wouldn't that be nice, as a leader, to always have a compass visible, to reaffirm that, yes, you are moving in the right direction, even when the situation becomes cloudy?

Often as a Pilot-Leader, your planned direction can take you towards some hazy horizons—uncertain market conditions, new technology, downsizing, mergers or acquisitions. To have the confidence that you will maintain a constant heading despite the "fog of battle" is reassuring.

As a leader, what or who is your compass? Maybe it is your relationship with your boss that provides that

feedback. Perhaps you have a mentor that you consult with routinely just to make sure you are on the right track. For some people it is the proverbial inner voice that guides them. For others, it is a set of guiding principles that keeps them aligned with their ultimate goal or destinations.

Many companies have adopted the practice of writing a company mission statement. This is written to give guidance during uncertain (cloudy) times; it is, in other words, a compass. Some companies take a laundry list approach to their mission statement and just add to information overload for the employees. Think about it—as a pilot, do you need ten compasses to tell you if you are still heading north? Keep it simple, and give your team members direction and simplicity. They will reward you with performance and loyalty.

Attitude Indicator. In a helicopter the attitude indicator is the largest instrument by far. Why? As a pilot you always need to know the attitude of the aircraft. Is it level, in a turn or headed for the ground? Most of the time the pilot can simply look outside to determine the aircraft's attitude, but in a cloud or at

night, you must know the attitude of the aircraft immediately.

As a Pilot-Leader, can you readily determine the attitudes of your teammates? The best way to gauge the attitudes of the team is through familiarity. Stand-off managers (those who believe that familiarity breeds contempt) will have trouble with this. As a Pilot-Leader, familiarity allows for an excellent attitude indicator. Knowing the baseline attitudes of each team member, you will always know when they are up and when they are down. Know them well enough to know their families, their hobbies and their passions. Know what is important to them, and what motivates them.

Wouldn't it be useful to sense the attitudes among your staff and to make corresponding control inputs before attitudes become a problem? Similarly, wouldn't you like to reinforce good attitudes and keep your team productive? Talk about developing situational awareness! You will be well on your way!

Some say that attitude and morale are the intangibles of leadership and that to monitor or even measure

these facets of a team is impossible. I certainly do not subscribe to this thought and neither should you! To leave such an important aspect of leadership and subsequent team performance to chance is as dangerous as flying blind! No helicopter pilot in his or her right mind would fly without an attitude indicator. No leader should trust morale or the attitudes of the team to chance either.

Another method for monitoring team attitudes toward their work environment is to implement a quarterly survey. Once the survey is given the first time, you could establish a baseline score for your team members' attitudes towards a variety of subjects including:

- information flow—are you being kept informed of changes?
- development—have you received feedback on your performance in the past 30 days?
- input—does your opinion count? Has one of your suggestions been implemented lately?
- job satisfaction—are you excited about work?

Record the results each time you collect the survey. By finding a problem with morale before it infects the team, you can keep team attitudes sky high instead of in a nosedive.

The Chairman of AES Corporation, an independent power producer with over one billion in annual sales, actually tracks his employees' job enjoyment. For a decade he has surveyed AES employees and his company's annual report itemizes the results. Employees consistently rank their level of fun at an average of eight out of a possible ten.

Group attitudes are just as important as individual attitudes. Because of their proximity in the work environment and simple human dynamics, people share attitudes like they do the common cold. Nothing can destroy the morale and subsequent performance of a team faster than an infectious bad attitude.

As CEO of Redmond Products (a multi-million-dollar hair care company), Tom Redmond called this infectious attitude "negativitis." He believed that "negativitis" affects the carrier's fellow workers, their friends, relatives and everyone with whom they

come into contact. He even encouraged his negative employees to go work for his competition!

If you don't monitor attitudes, your entire team can become infected, and it takes time and effort to repair the damage—time and effort better spent on winning more market share. For this reason, it is imperative that you continue to monitor attitudes and correct the situation at the first sign of problems. Leaving a bad attitude to right itself is a recipe for disaster! As in flying, keep an eye on your team's attitude indicator, make necessary control inputs and watch your team fly!

Ready to soar

Now that you know how to "fly," you can accumulate flight time (flying experience) and as you do so, you can use your Pilot Vision to build your situational awareness. The Pilot-Leaders with situational awareness are those that gain enough experience to trust that inner voice or that "gut feeling." Situational awareness resembles the fabled "women's intuition." Learn to trust that inner voice and routinely act on it. Again, experience is the only way to hone this attribute. The more you follow your inner voice, the more you will learn to trust it and the

more you will find yourself situationally aware and ready to soar. You'll be ready, willing and able to take action.

Pilot-Leader empowering questions

How can you develop your situational awareness?

What additional leadership roles could you take on to gain this experience?

Do you monitor your team's attitude? If so, how?

Do you spend 90 percent of your time thinking of a solution and only 10 percent of your time fixing things or the other way around?

Has your inner voice or intuition provided you with the answers and have you ignored them? Why?

4
The Power in Planning

"Fail to plan
and you are planning
to fail."
Anonymous

 4

The Power in Planning

Planning skills separate good pilots from the rare, exceptional pilot.

An exceptional pilot can rapidly collect, evaluate and process reams of information in any given situation and put together a workable plan.

Short-term slowdown, long-term gain

A fundamental planning principle for both pilots and leaders can be found in the saying: "Slow down to speed up."

Though it may appear to be contradictory, to be a Pilot-Leader it is often necessary to slow down, get the needed information, make a plan and then take off.

Imagine two pilots preparing for flights from Los

Angeles to New York City. One jumps in the cockpit, starts the engines and takes off without planning the flight. The second pilot begins by checking the weather, inspecting the aircraft and getting everyone organized for the flight. Sure the second pilot is behind the first pilot, but because the second pilot slowed down, the aircraft will be able to speed up later. For example, a fuel stop won't be needed since extra fuel was added in preparation for a head wind.

Because of planning skills and the investment in a few minutes before the flight, the second pilot will be able to take advantage of a good tail wind at a higher altitude. Regardless, slowing down to plan will allow you to speed up later when it counts.

On the ground, successful pilots are ruthless in their attention to detail in flight planning. They use a checklist with checkpoints, which are locations clearly identifiable from the air and associated with timelines. They double and triple check planning figures and then have these figures reviewed by other pilots. They know that to overlook any detail is to invite problems.

With a plan you are able to move in a direction to capitalize on opportunities. Earl Nightingale once said, "Luck is where opportunity meets preparation." Think of your goal setting and "flight planning" as your preparation. When the opportunity presents itself, you will be ready.

Pilot-Leaders use planning in three important areas: goals, time and contingencies.

Goal planning

Linda Finch (U.S. pilot, adventurer, businesswoman, entrepreneur and mother) flew around the world in 1997 completing the famed Amelia Earhart flight of sixty years earlier.

How did Finch do it? She began with a plan. Her planning included linking together short-term goals for each leg of her historic flight. The first leg of the flight was from Oakland to Monterey, an easy but a necessary first step. Once she arrived safely, she knew that each future leg would also have to be taken one at a time and the cumulative result would be to encircle the globe.

She demonstrated that to accomplish anything of merit, you must break a long-term goal into many short-term goals. By the way, she carried with her on her flight a book of stories by the late Norman Vincent Peale, the master of goal-oriented thinking and planning.

The Mercury flights were a necessary first step for our space program. They opened the door and gave NASA and our country the momentum that quite literally carried us to the moon.

All Pilot-Leaders plan both short- and long-term goals that have the three following characteristics:

1. Goals should be *quantifiable* and therefore, clearly measurable.

2. All goals should be *written*.

3. For goals to be effective, they must have a *timeline* attached to them.

Quantifiable goals
Selecting a goal that can be measured and is readily identifiable insures that you and your team have a

specific goal to shoot for. A generalized goal of increased revenue may produce results, but a more specific goal of one million dollars in sales revenue for the third quarter is a checkpoint that can be seen and for which strategies can be developed.

Don't underestimate the importance of specific, short-term goals. Just as a pilot chooses checkpoints to show whether the aircraft is on track toward its ultimate destination, you also must have a method to see your progress and to determine whether you need to change direction, speed up or seek out additional resources.

Written goals

Can you imagine a pilot of a commercial airliner planning a flight across the country but not writing down the route? No! The route is written, well-defined and never just entrusted to memory. To reach the destination, the checkpoints must be recorded. The same is true for you as a leader.

Chicken Soup coauthor Mark Victor Hansen says, "Don't just think it, ink it." That little ditty serves as a great reminder that you must record your goals,

thoughts and plans in order to make them most effective.

In 1953, Yale University conducted a study of its graduating seniors. They found that though many of the students had a vision for their future, only two percent had a written plan for their careers. Only two percent had taken the time to record short- and long-range goals to take them to their ultimate destination.

While most of the graduates had a vision that they wanted to be doctors, lawyers or investment bankers, only two percent had thought out a plan for realizing their visions. Twenty years later, Yale commissioned a study to examine the performance of the 1953 graduating class. Predictably, the two percent who had a vision plus goals and a written plan were more successful in terms of salary and positions attained.

Critics of this checkpoint planning approach often complain that it is too rigid and that it does not give you enough freedom to change course. On the contrary, with a written plan, you now have a basis from which to deviate.

Goals with timelines

A goal is nothing more than a wish unless you establish a timeline to achieve it. Timelines or deadlines create useful stress. Useful stress is what gets us up every morning and causes us to take action. As you see your deadline approaching, redouble your efforts and cross that checkpoint with ease and ahead of schedule, if possible.

What about obstacles?

In setting and achieving goals, you will run into occasional roadblocks. The solution to these obstacles can be found again in the pilot planning sequence. If the pilot foresees potential obstacles or even encounters them, the pilot has two options: continue down the same course or make a course deviation. Does the pilot of a Boeing 777 then just simply fly around the storm ahead? No, a pilot sets up a series of new checkpoints that will guide the aircraft around the obstacle and then back on course.

Masters of time planning

Grounded in solid planning skills, the best pilots in the airways are the ones who are exceptional time

managers. The worst pilots seem to allow time to dictate their actions.

The best pilots in commercial aviation routinely arrive and depart on time.

For America's secret commando pilots, time is everything. If you could look in the cockpit of their specially modified black helicopters, you wouldn't believe your eyes—just count the number of clocks. Up on the forward panel there are two analog clocks and two digital clocks. Down on the center console there are two more digital stand-alone readouts. On the infra-red monitor displays in front of them there are two more. On each pilot's wrist, there is a digital watch.

Why this obsession with time? The measure of success to which each commando pilot adheres is a narrow margin: plus or minus thirty seconds from the designated time. That is their standard to deliver ordnance and secret warriors to various targets worldwide. Embassies, hostage situations, car chases, you name it: if they are not there on time, they are considered a failure. No asset is more important to

them and critical to mission success than time.

What do the best pilots do that allows them to arrive at a destination at a predetermined time, even to the second? What secret do they possess? It is the secret of reverse time planning and it is a hallmark of Pilot-Leaders.

Reverse time planning
It is really quite simple but powerful in its application. I speak from firsthand experience having flown as one of the masters of reverse time planning — America's most elite helicopter pilots, the "Nightstalkers" of Task Force 160. These pilots guarantee their secret warrior "customers" that they will deliver them anywhere in the world plus or minus thirty seconds! No package delivery company in the world can hope to live up to that standard.

The Nightstalkers owe their success to the fact that they integrate reverse planning into every facet of their operations. For example, if a "customer" tells them they want to be on a rooftop of a specific building at 2:30 a.m., then that is where they begin: at the end. All planning revolves around delivery of

the customer at the prescribed time and then is planned in reverse. All time planning is done with the end in mind. The pilots treat each second as an asset, wasting none.

For Nightstalkers, time management is a science. For Pilot-Leaders, it's more of an art. You need to know what good time management is for your business, which probably isn't quite as exacting as it is for a Nightstalker.

Everyone on earth is given the same 24 hours in a day. As a successful Pilot-Leader you can do more with your time than others. This includes investing time in planning your day/week/month/year in advance. Trying to decide what is important while immersed in the day is like trying to plan a flight while flying. It can be done and many people live their lives this way, moment to moment. However, if you plan out your allotted 24 hours, you will consistently turn out better results. How?

Like a pilot, you begin with the end in mind, keeping your goals, vision and your destination in sight. As a result, you will invest quality time in what is

most important to you. The key is knowing what those things are.

Your "flight plan"

Before climbing in the cockpit, all pilots are required to write and file a "flight plan." This is a detailed account of who they are, where they are going and how they intend to get there. Consider entries in your daily planner or organizer like filing a flight plan. To operate without it is to trust your already overburdened mind with too many details.

The best personal organizing tool that I have seen (and believe me, I've tried many!) is made by Priority Manager™ (http://www.priority-management.com). It has several features that I like including the durable paper card stock (which prevents the pages from pulling out) and the short-term, mid-term and long-range goals planning section. An added benefit is that the company teaches you how to use the system during a half-day seminar. These seminars are available internationally.

The time you invest learning how to best use a system and stay organized will pay big dividends down

the road.

Contingency planning

Top-notch pilots also plan for every conceivable contingency by conducting a "what-if" drill. For a pilot it sounds like this:

- What if our fuel burn rate is higher than normal, will we still make it to our destination?

- What if we encounter head winds that slow our progress, will we have to make an en-route stop?

- What if we encounter thunderstorms, can we divert around them?

For a Pilot-Leader in business, a "what-if" drill is very similar:

- What if this project costs more than our predictions, can we still complete the project?

- What if the first phase takes longer than anticipated, can the project still finish on time?

- What if my lead sales representative is sick or otherwise diverted, who can best replace my sales rep in front of the customer?

This is called contingency planning and is an integral part of planning that is so crucial to leadership success. It also prepares a leader for the inevitable "destination change." If you adequately perform pre-mission planning, you will be capable of solving problems with smooth transitions that may go unnoticed by your customers.

Overcoming Murphy's Law

You've probably heard of at least one Murphy's Law, the most famous one being: "If anything can go wrong, it will." Through detailed planning and preparation, Pilot-Leaders prepare for "Murphy" because they must rise above problems and be the master of their surroundings.

Pilots, and hence Pilot-Leaders, don't buy into Murphy. Pilots routinely "break" Murphy's Law and replace it with the much more powerful Pilot-Leaders' Golden Rule: Control your environment.

As a leader, you are responsible for everything your team does or doesn't do. In this era of downsizing and zero defects, do you think for a moment that your customers will write off your mistakes to Murphy?

Visualize contingencies

An important part of contingency planning that many leave out is visualization. This powerful tool allows you to see and experience your plan long before you implement it. Military pilots have been doing this for years, picturing their targets before they fly their mission.

Today they add to the realism by using state-of-the-art simulators to "live" their plan long before they actually fly it. Commercial pilots spend time each year flying into challenging weather conditions in the safety of the simulator. Here they learn to visualize a calm, by-the-book response to a real emergency that can save the lives of their passengers.

Implement visualization in your team planning sessions. Visualization can often uncover contingencies or obstacles that you may have missed.

Pilots are notorious for their attention to detail and it is never more evident than when planning a flight. After looking over the aircraft, the first stop is the planning station. Pulling out the map covering the route, the pilot will check to insure that there are no known obstacles along the route. And a wise leader will do the same. Anything you as a leader can do to reduce risks to you and your team will prove beneficial. Contingency planning is essential for your success.

Pilot-Leader empowering questions

How often do you rely on others to do your critical thinking and planning? Are they even qualified?

How much time (if any) do you dedicate to preplanning your key meetings, presentations or sales calls? Do you use a checklist to avoid omitting key points?

Do you conduct contingency planning to avoid "surprises?"

Do you have both short- and long-term goals?

Do you visualize your plans before implementation to improve your results?

Do you use an effective daily planner? Do your teammates or staff use one?

How could "slowing down to speed up" help you achieve better results?

Do you and your team have a consistently high standard of "on-time" delivery to the customer?

Do you have a flight plan for success?

5
Soaring with Technology

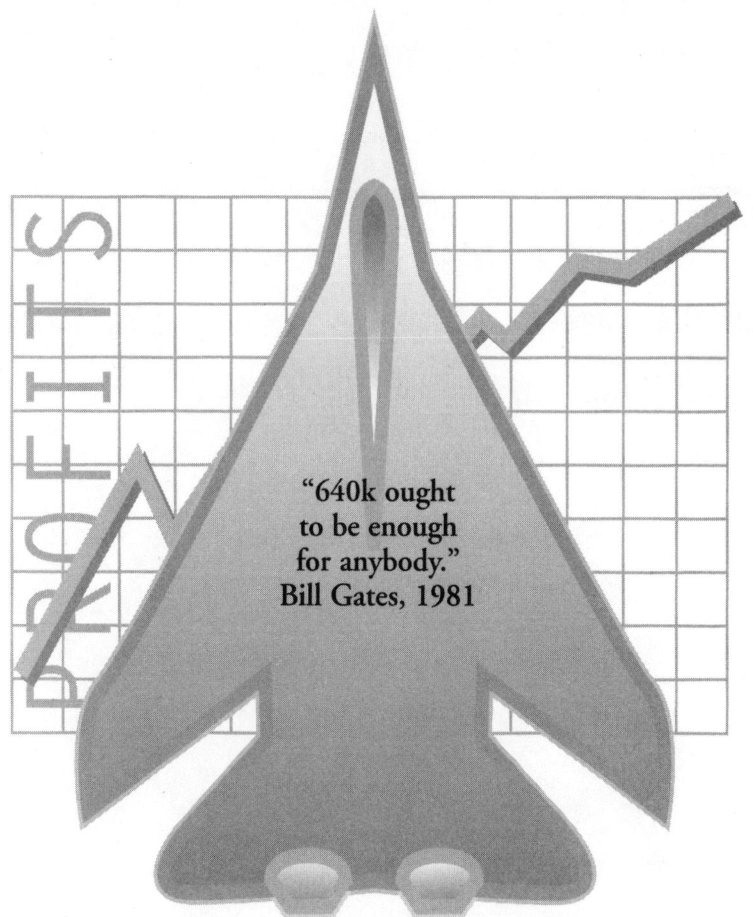

5

Soaring with Technology

No one could have predicted the relentless march of technology that we are currently experiencing. It is a powerful foundation upon which the U.S. and much of the world economy now rests.

Technology has pervaded all aspects of our daily and business lives and has also changed the aviation industry almost beyond recognition.

Today the best pilots are masters of technology, not slaves to it. Today's cockpits are filled with myriad CRTs (cathode ray tubes), MFDs (multifunctional displays) and perhaps more computer chips than an Intel assembly line. With the passing of pioneering astronaut Alan Shepard, we are reminded of just how far our technology has come since 1961. Shepard's flight lasted 15 minutes, while today, astronauts

travel in reusable shuttles and live in space for months on end, a feat made possible by advancing technology.

Today's best pilots have grasped this high-tech trend by the throttle and stayed ahead of it using automation to make them better and safer pilots. Global Positioning System (GPS) satellite computers allow pilots to pinpoint their exact position relative to their destination and more importantly, relative to other aircraft. Computerized flight controls allow for the effortless control of larger and more complex aircraft.

Aircraft can now be flown safely in weather that would have been impassable without computerized onboard Doppler radar, precision approach computers and infrared cameras. Those who don't use this technology are being left on the ground shaking their heads. Why should technology be important to you as a leader? Read on.

Using technology to increase wealth

In his groundbreaking book *Unlimited Wealth*, Paul Pilzer puts forth a remarkable premise—a modern theory of alchemy that works. Unlike the alchemists

in ancient times who unsuccessfully tried to turn base metals into gold, with technology we now have the ability to create wealth where there was none before. Pilzer asserts that $W=PT^n$ where "W" stands for wealth, which is the product of physical resources (P) and technology (T). In his equation the "n" next to the "T" is the power of the technology. The higher the level of technology, the greater the wealth that's produced.

A striking example of Pilzer's theory is the use of technology to increase the wealth of oil reserves. As the last of the baby boomers, I grew up during the oil crisis of the early 1970s. This was a time when gas rationing and double-digit inflation were normal.

Headlines predicted a depleted oil supply by the end of the 20th century. Doomsayers, however, failed to predict that technology would help us find additional oil reserves and even improve our efficiency in using fossil fuels. Now, using super-computing models, better drilling equipment and other high-tech tools, the world's known oil reserves have increased. What changed in Pilzer's "wealth" formula above? The level of physical resources remained

virtually a constant. What created wealth was the exponential increase in technology to locate previously unknown resources.

Using technology to develop products or processes

Today, it can really pay off to use technology in business. Let's look at, for example, how the combined genius of Boeing and its numerous suppliers and vendors used computer technology for communication (groupware and an intranet) to create the world's first completely computer-designed commercial aircraft: the Boeing 777.

Boeing used the Internet to share design changes and test the impact of such moves before final production. In fact, the aircraft was flown in virtual wind tunnels even before any type of scale model was produced. The cost savings that resulted from this kind of technological innovation were enormous. The leaders at Boeing embraced technology and mastered its use as a design tool.

Here's another example of maximizing technology to design aircraft. Aerospace engineers have been trying

to perfect the concept of the "tilt-rotor" commuter aircraft for almost forty years with little success. A tilt-rotor commuter aircraft would combine a helicopter's vertical takeoff and landing with the speed and range of an airplane.

Recent technological innovations have pushed this idea from the concept stage onto center stage. New technology in fly-by-wire controls and composite materials have now lightened the aircraft so that a tilt-rotor can now carry a respectable payload (early models could only carry a pilot and copilot).

Bell Helicopters and Boeing, the coproducers of this unique aircraft, stand ready to turn the aviation industry upside down. While others said it couldn't be done (including the U.S. Government who cut funding for the project twice), Bell and Boeing researched, developed and then implemented the necessary technological advances.

Tilt-rotor will revolutionize the commercial aviation industry just as the jet engine did. Soon you will be able to catch a tilt-rotor, 24-passenger turbo-prop from downtown, fly faster than today's commuter

prop-planes and land in, not outside, a city of your choosing.

Are you staying on top of the latest breakthroughs in your industry?

The potential downside of technology

Here's a word of warning: if you allow yourself to be caught up in technology for technology's sake and not as a tool, you can actually lose productivity and risk losing control of your "flight" environment. A quick review of many of the latest commercial airline tragedies reveals how technology can overcomplicate the simplest of tasks.

A crash of a modern passenger jetliner in Latin America resulted from a pilot typing in the wrong approach heading (he hit the wrong key on the keyboard). Predictably the aircraft did what it was told.

There are other dangers as well. Relying too much on automation can take you out of the decision loop. Pilots now have to work harder than ever to remain an integral part of the loop in their automated cock-

pits. As a leader you must fight to stay in the loop even as many of the everyday tasks around you become automated.

We must use technology, not be used by it.

How are we being used by technology? When we put off calling a client because our electronic organizers are down, we are a slave to technology. When we spend critical office time checking and answering irrelevant intraoffice e-mail instead of solving design problems on a product, we have missed the point of automation. When we are routinely unable to access critical data on the server because the "system" is down, we need to rethink our reliance on technology.

There's another trap to avoid as we create the mythical paperless office: over-engineering. With the current pace of technological changes, it is easy to over-engineer the simplest of tasks. (Need a phone number? Forget the little black book. Let me look it up on my pocket PDA!)

The "space pen" is an example of "complication by

technology." Engineered and funded by NASA during the space race of the 1960s, this technological marvel could write in the zero gravity of outer space. Using a team of engineers, computer-aided design and a substantial budget, the U.S. team produced a one-of-a-kind instrument.

There was an alternative. Faced with the same task, the Soviet Union accomplished the same objective at a fraction of the cost—they used a pencil!

A good friend served with the British military during the 1991 Gulf War. During the allied offensive on Iraq's retreating forces, he happened upon a British tank crew who had stopped during the height of the advance. Puzzled, he approached the idling armored vehicle and asked them why they weren't moving with the rest of the column. Much to my friend's amazement the tank commander replied, "Our GPS computer is not working, so we can't move." The tank crew had become so reliant on the GPS that they equated a broken GPS with a broken tank. Although they had maps, compasses and a fully functioning armored combat vehicle (not to mention their brains!), they stopped moving forward. Do not

let the lure of high technology lull you into a similar trap.

I have even heard the following disturbing exchange between service sector employees:

> "Where are you going? It is only 9 a.m."
> "I'm leaving for the day. I can't do anything because my computer is down."

What is "down" is this person's initiative and drive. This is too much reliance upon the computer to do the work and thinking.

Many people in today's workforce do not distinguish between thinking and computing. The truth is, computers today are incapable of real creative thought, brainstorming or counseling of fellow workers. As a Pilot-Leader, your most important tool is your brain.

The pace of technological change is accelerating. Moore's Law (computing power doubles every 12 months) insures that it will continue. What remains a challenge will be your ability to harness the coming

tools and keep your creative thought sharp. As a Pilot-Leader, you need to stay technologically oriented but not at the expense of your critical thinking and leadership skills.

Pilot-Leader empowering questions

Are you staying abreast of the latest technological advances in your field? How can technology help you work more efficiently or increase your wealth?

Will you be able to position your company or team to take advantage of these changes? Will a competitor get there first?

What technological enhancements have you employed to improve your corporate vision? What technology are your competitors using?

Have computers or automation ceased becoming workplace tools and overcomplicated your life?

6
Communicating Your Vision

"I know
you believe
you understand
what you think
I said, but I am not
sure you realize what you
heard is not what I meant."
Anonymous

PROFITS

6

Communicating Your Vision

Clear communication for pilots is as essential as the "wind beneath their wings" (actually, it is the wind over the wings that produces the lift, but that is another story).

If you talk to a pilot on an aircraft's radio, you will notice well-chosen words and crystal clear communication. A good pilot is an effective communicator. Can you imagine flying in an aircraft with a pilot who could not communicate with the air traffic controller? The pilot would probably have trouble taking off and landing. Would you want to fly with that pilot?

We can communicate an idea around the world in seventy seconds, but as Charles Kettering once said, "It sometimes takes years for an idea to get through

one-quarter inch of human skull."

Pilot-Leaders must be able to communicate with both their internal team and external suppliers and customers. As a business leader, you must be able to effectively communicate your vision in order to build support for your product or business.

Someone once described for me the role of a leader this way. As an expeditionary team makes its way through the jungle, the leader is not the one swinging the blade, making the way clear. No, that is the "manager's" role. The leader is ahead up in a tree scouting out the best route and communicating the information to the team. The leader is in a position to guide the team toward the goal.

The challenge for a leader is to convey this vision to his or her team. I once heard a speaker say, "A vision is like a baby: easy to conceive, yet difficult to deliver!" How accurate.

As a Pilot-Leader you can often gauge your abilities or success by how well your team understands your vision. Just ask them. Do they understand your

vision completely? How often do you reveal to them your strategic plans for the future of the team? Do they understand why they are moving in that chosen direction? If not, then the fault can only rest with you. If you keep a vision to yourself, you have no vision, only a wish. Inform and empower your team and watch them soar with you.

Communications during a crisis

Although the early barnstorming pilots could get by without air-to-air and air-to-ground radio equipment, in today's congested skies, pilots must be capable of clear and concise broadcasts to neighboring pilots as well as to ground controllers. In the event that a commercial passenger airplane loses communication contact with the ground controller, the situation is declared an emergency and handled with increased priority. Aircraft are rerouted and runways are cleared until the aircraft can be brought back to the airport.

Military pilots also put a premium on being able to communicate clearly with each other. The military has learned this lesson the hard way. A contributing cause for the failure of the Iranian hostage rescue

attempt of 1980, for example, was a breakdown in communications among the helicopters, the on-ground commanders directing the mission and other participating agencies.

As in business, when communications fail in times of crisis, the results are as predictable as the setting of the sun.

Calm in the eye of the storm

Pilots must be capable of communicating with passengers, crew members and air traffic controllers even while problems are occurring. Pilots are drilled on keeping passengers calm, communicating the situation to controllers and calmly reacting to the situation. Anything less can spell disaster. For both pilots and leaders, poor communication skills will worsen a situation. Good communications can help save you and your team.

During a rough financial ride, your ability to calm your team and communicate the situation to those who can provide help will be of most importance. So when your customers, suppliers or investors call, you will be ready to reassure them of a safe landing.

When all else fails, simplify!

Prior to the start of the Gulf War ground war, the coalition forces built an intricate matrix of radio frequencies protected by even more complex encryption devices to prevent the Iraqi forces from eavesdropping on friendly aircraft and ground troops. Unfortunately, this complexity made it often impossible for allied aircraft to communicate with friendly ground forces below. Incorrect frequencies or even incorrect decryption codes prevented air and ground forces from working together.

That didn't last long; pilots and ground forces migrated to a common "emergency" frequency and turned off the encryption. Once the word was disseminated that only one frequency was needed, the war moved on. Sometimes simpler is better.

As a Pilot-Leader be wary of overcomplicating your communications.

"Hot mike"

Be wary, also, of the hot-mic (pronounced "hot mike") which is a radio term for a microphone switch that is stuck in the "on" position. When this

happens, you begin to pick up unintended conversations from the cockpit and worse yet, no one else on that channel can talk! The communications are essentially shut down and you may have to listen to a conversation about what someone had for lunch instead of what could be vital information.

How do your communications get shut down where you live and work? Which people do you perceive as having a hot-mic, who have the communications all going one way? How could you reopen that channel and thus improve communications?

Pilot-Leader empowering questions

How could you simplify and improve your business communications?

How are your speaking skills? Can you inspire your teammates with the right words? Have you considered joining a public speaking organization like Toastmasters?

How could you improve your writing skills?

How do you respond in a crisis?

7
The Power of Knowledge

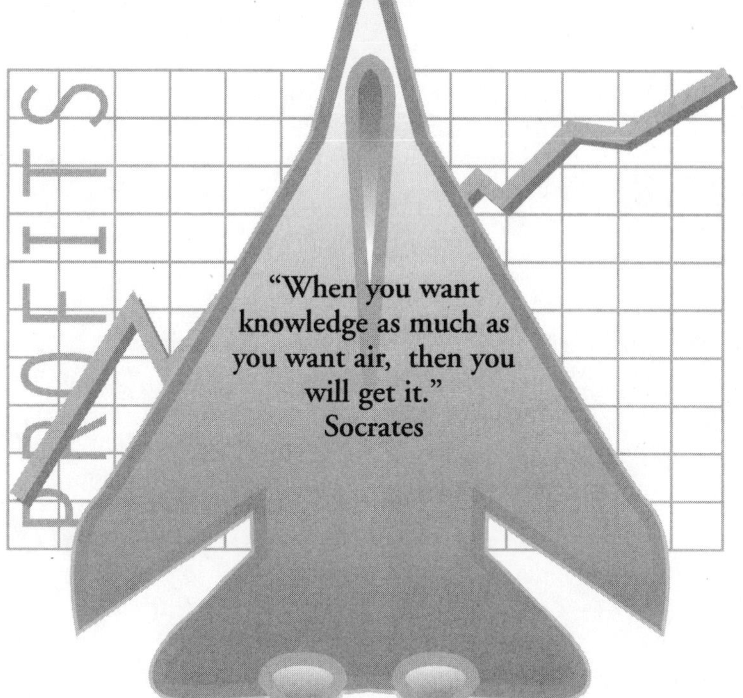

7
The Power of Knowledge

All military and commercial pilots are required by law to take a specified minimum of continuing education classes each year. These courses help pilots stay on top of the industry and the myriad changes that could affect the safe operation of their aircraft. In my opinion, the law that requires these classes is unnecessary. Pilots know the importance of constant learning. In an industry where ignorance spells death, pilots would take classes even if it were not required. The best Pilot-Leaders feel the same way about education in their businesses.

I say all this despite the fact that many pilots, entrepreneurs and leaders achieve greatness without the benefit of an MBA or other graduate degree. One only has to look at the success of Thomas Edison (three months of formal schooling), or Soichiro

Honda (thrown out of his university) to see that there is often something far greater than formal education. Don't think that these cases are relegated to the precomputer era. Just look at billionaire Bill Gates. He dropped out of Harvard before he could be awarded his undergraduate degree.

What these people did grasp, though, was the power of knowledge attained through continual self-development. They realized that to restrict their learning to the confines of an educational institution was to relinquish control over their learning and development. To allow formal education to be your sole source of knowledge is to be forever two-dimensional. Self-development requires ongoing learning to provide the third dimension essential to Pilot-Leaders.

By the way, ongoing professional development for your entire team can be a great way to improve morale. Better than cash rewards (readily spent), better than time off (goes by too fast), good training stays with them for life! Send your teammates to a seminar or help them enroll in continuing education. The effects last longer and you will see morale sky-

rocket.

The world's best pilots are committed to the idea of ongoing learning and self-development. Their lives and the lives of their crew and passengers depend on it. Shouldn't you take a similar attitude toward honing your skills? Here's what the best pilots do and what you should do, too.

Annual comprehensive skills check-up

Every year, pilots are required to demonstrate to an instructor their proficiency in basic piloting skills. The rationale is: if you can perform on demand, under the stress of a flight evaluation with basic tasks, you will have a firm foundation during an actual emergency.

Outside evaluations are much more revealing than a self-critique. Have someone from outside your team or business give you an honest evaluation of your leadership skills and the performance of the business each year. Since this is not the time for stroking egos, avoid going to your friends for this type of feedback. Select someone who can be "brutally honest" and provide you with constructive criticism as well as

specific information on what to change or improve.

Annual comprehensive medical evaluation
Never allow concern or lack of knowledge about your health to interfere with your ability to lead your team. Get a qualified opinion, take any recommended action steps and quit worrying about it! Then like a well-armed warrior, you can tackle your life's work with confidence. As French philosopher Jean Jacques Rousseau said: "When the body is weak, it takes over command. When strong, it obeys."

Periodic industry updates
The technology in aviation is changing rapidly. The cockpit, the flight environment and even customer requests are becoming more and more technical and automated. The best pilots refuse to be left behind and therefore, stay ahead of the changes. As a leader, you must have access to the latest trends of your industry. What periodicals do you get? Do you use Internet news "hounds" to search out the latest information for your industry? What seminars do you and your team attend to keep up to date?

Your "PIF"

In every planning room of every flight unit in our nation's military there is required reading for every pilot that takes to the skies. This "Pilot Information File," or PIF as it is known, is mandatory reading for all pilots before they get into the cockpit. The PIF contains up-to-the-minute data and articles from the world of aviation. It might be a listing of the latest hazards to flight (weather balloons, bird migrations or gliders) or a summary of the latest accident investigation. In the PIF one might also find information on the latest technological advances for a particular aircraft.

Regardless of the content, the rational for the PIF is simple: pilots know that to be the best, they have to be armed with the latest information. This data may indeed save lives. It is the information deemed most critical to their profession and they feed on it every day. Do you have a similar source of information for yourself and others in your office? How do you stay on top of the industry in which you work? If it's in sales, then include the latest sales strategies or an article from *Success Magazine* for your team. Are the latest sales figures in? Then publish them in your

own PIF ("Professional Information File") for all to see. Did somebody have a particular measure of success (or failure) with a client? Share it with the group. Information hoarded today is surely not power. By the way, groupware and intranets are great methods for disseminating your new PIF to your team.

Monthly "brain trust" meetings

Pilots routinely gather to swap lessons they have learned or trends they see in aviation. As a pilot I made it a point to meet monthly with pilots, engineers, meteorologists and air traffic controllers to broaden my perspective on my profession. Assembling your own brain trust in and out of your industry can provide you with a source of emerging trends. However, don't go to these meetings empty handed. Your chosen colleagues will be in search of new information as well.

The power of knowledge in a crisis

There are only a few things pilots will commit to memory rather than use a checklist and that's only when a situation dictates that they take immediate action or risk losing control of the aircraft.

The need for immediate action does not happen often. More often than not, the pilot has an opportunity to analyze the situation and make a smooth recovery.

Furthermore, a capable pilot will have brought a checklist that provides step-by-step procedures to take in the event of an emergency. These steps can range from the simple—land as soon as possible—to the complex—battery off, generators off, pull circuit breakers, adjust airspeed and land as soon as practicable.

In either case, very few aircraft emergencies require immediate action. Why? Although the first human instinct is to attempt to take full control of the aircraft, many times it's only a small part that is causing the trouble. You have a much better chance of surviving if you take a step back, analyze the situation, gather all the data and follow your checklist. That's why you carry it as a pilot. That's why you need one as a Pilot-Leader.

I know of no Pilot-Leader who has all the answers. But I know of many who keep at hand the resources

to deal with everyday as well as special challenges. It helps to have many of the answers readily available in a time of crisis and for everyday operations.

When a pilot uses a checklist, it serves not as a crutch, but as a tool to help the pilot see things that might be missed in times of crisis. Who can forget the power of the emergency checklist that saved the lives of the Apollo 13 crew?

The power of pilot error

The number one cause of aircraft accidents is also the number one cause of business failings. According to FAA statistics, the number one cause of aircraft accidents (or incidents as they like to call them) is not material or component failure. That ranks fourth. It is not sabotage, although those types of incidents seem to get the most publicity today. No, the number one cause of aircraft incidents in the nation (and the world) is pilot error.

How does this relate to you as a leader? According to Small Business Administration statistics, the number one cause of business failures is not market dynamics, hostile takeovers or union walkouts. No, the

number one reason for businesses failing in our country is poor leadership. Despite all our training, charisma, sales savvy and technology, most businesses, teams or staffs that fail this year will fail because of something the leader did or failed to do. So stop looking around when something goes wrong, and look in the mirror. Chances are the problem is with you. Remember as a leader, you are the pilot, and you are sitting in the pilot's seat. But, you say, "I didn't see that market downturn coming," or "How could I have predicted that my CFO would run us into the red?" Good questions. Let's look to a helicopter pilot for answers.

How does a helicopter pilot see the mountains while flying in the clouds? Clairvoyance? Gut instinct? Luck, or any of the other oft attributed success factors? Hardly.

How does the pilot know when an engine is about to overheat and start a fire when the engine is located six feet behind and three feet above? Omniscience? ESP? No way!

A helicopter is designed around the pilot, as most

businesses or teams should be structured around the leader. The pilot's cockpit is a mixture of controls, indicators and navigation equipment which enable the pilot to guide the aircraft through the air, avoiding obstacles and incidents. As a leader, you need to do the same thing: surround yourself with the people and data that give you the ability to know what's happening now and what is going to happen down the road.

Let's look back at those pilot error accidents. Records show that the gauges were probably operating correctly and the controls were functioning normally. So what could have been the problem? In many cases, the pilot disregarded the instruments. Perhaps the pilot became fixated on one indication to the detriment of the other indications. Maybe the pilot over-controlled (micromanaged), putting too many inputs into the controls, thereby nullifying the aerodynamic effects of the parts of the helicopter that were keeping the aircraft in the air. Do any of these causes sound like they could occur in the workplace? They can and they do, resulting in business failings, poor quarterly earnings and unhappy stockholders. Knowledge of how accidents and setbacks occur combined

with knowing what to do when they do happen is vital to your team and business survival.

Pilot-Leader empowering questions

When was the last time you invested in your future and enrolled in a seminar or continuing education class? When was the last time you sent your team?

When was the last time you had an external evaluation of your team or leadership? Would an "outside-the-company" perspective uncover some potential problems and identify some solutions?

Do you have a professional development reading program for you and your team?

When was your last physical?

8
Flying with Trust

"As a rule, men worry
more about what they
can't see than about
what they can."
Julius Caesar

8

Flying with Trust

Thirty feet from death. Thirty feet above the sea. A black helicopter is invisible at night as it skims the waves and approaches the shoreline at speeds in excess of 200 miles per hour. America's secret warrior helicopter pilots are trained to conduct this maneuver by using NightVision Goggles (NVGs) and instruments designed to keep them and their aircraft out of the drink.

What is the most important element for them as they steer their $30 million aircraft mere seconds from plunging into the dark sea? Trust. Trust in a little three-inch gauge that stares them in the face from the instrument panel. The gauge, called a "radar altimeter," gives the pilots a digital readout of their exact height above the water. The gauge must be calibrated, so they must trust the mechanic who installed it. The gauge must be accurate, so they must trust the manufacturer.

The pilot on the controls cannot see the instrument, so the pilot must rely on the copilot to monitor it. The copilot is not on the controls, so the copilot must trust the pilot's skills. If the aircraft begins to settle, they will all be wet before the copilot can get to the controls anyway. By the way, the passengers in the back cannot see what is happening and have no influence on the situation. So they must trust the pilots, instruments and manufacturers and hope that everyone has done their job. What level of trust exists in your organization?

Without trust, most aircraft would never leave the ground. Without trusting the laws of aerodynamics, the crew and the pilot would never feel confident getting out of the hangar. Even more confidence is required once the aircraft is in flight, when the pilot must trust that the cockpit indicators are providing correct data, even when the pilot cannot see the horizon!

Real trust is a round-trip ticket on a two-way street

Teams must operate similarly. As a Pilot-Leader, you will never accomplish the difficult tasks ahead without trusting your team. Your team will not trust you

as a leader unless you trust them. It is definitely a leap of faith. But like a pilot's trust in the crew and ground support, it is an essential leap, provided you've done your homework.

To establish trust, you need to show you are committed to the development of your team. In aircraft terms, you need to provide for the "maintenance" of your team. Periodic and thorough, your personnel maintenance plan should be as comprehensive as any aircraft maintenance plan. High performance aircraft require certain actions from trained technicians daily, weekly, monthly and also after certain stressful situations (for example: hot, sandy or saltwater exposure). The same is true for your team. You can set up your maintenance plan with relative ease, but the key is implementing it.

Action	*Frequency*
Personal goal setting, review	Monthly
Professional development	Every other month
Staff meeting	Weekly
Morale check	Daily

As a Pilot-Leader, your optimal performance comes only after learning to trust your team. Naturally, it's essential to have the right type of people. Conrad Hilton, founder of Hilton Hotels Corporation, built his empire by "choosing competent people, placing them in key positions and trusting their judgment implicitly." Without this trust, he could never have headed a hotel chain that today stretches around the world in 50 countries.

Trust in human dynamics

After spending many hours in the air and classroom, a pilot develops an understanding and level of trust in the principles of aerodynamics. These principles can be found in Newton's Laws of Motion. These laws are irrefutable, nonnegotiable and irrevocable, affecting all aspects of flight.

As a Pilot-Leader, you must also trust in similar principles of human dynamics. For example, Newton's Third Law pertains to life and leadership as much as it does to physics. This is the law of action and reaction. In a biblical context it is described as follows: "As ye sow, so shall ye reap."

As a Pilot-Leader, you can trust in the fact that you

and your team will reap a bountiful harvest, provided that you plant, cultivate, weed and nurture your business. Trying to make the quick buck, win the lottery or have it all can only lead to unrealized dreams.

You cannot get something for nothing. You can trust in the knowledge that your positive actions should result in positive results.

Earned trust

Newton's law is essential for gaining and maintaining the trust so vital to your success as a Pilot-Leader. In addition to this law of human dynamics, trust is built upon the foundation of the six other pilot secrets we've explored in this book: Pilot Vision, Situational Awareness, the Power in Planning, Soaring with Technology, Communicating Your Vision and the Power of Knowledge. With this grounding, trust should kick in. But if you flounder in any of these areas, don't expect trust to magically bail you out. Trust must be earned through hard work by you and every team member. It must not be blind; rather it should emerge naturally as you acquire "flight time" experience and exercise true Pilot Vision.

Pilot-Leader empowering questions

Are you micromanaging your team? How much more efficient could you be with your staff by empowering them through trust?

Do you understand and apply human dynamics in your business?

How else can you build trust between you and your team?

Do your employees trust that you will safely pilot the team to success?

9
Putting It All Together

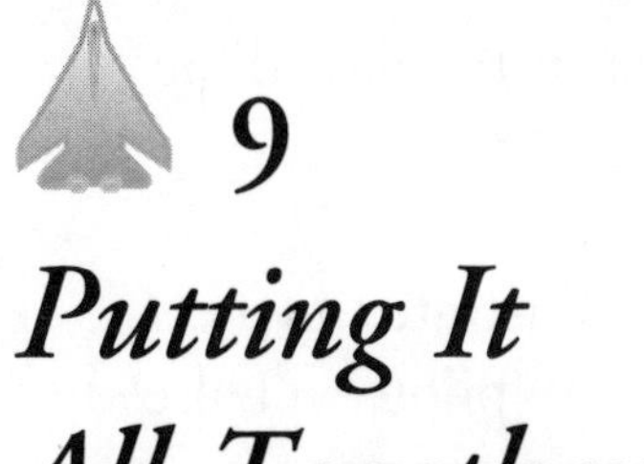

9 Putting It All Together

Becoming a pilot is a daunting task. Not everyone can pass the tests, summon the courage, gain the skills and apply themselves to take to the skies. But I can assure you there are few things in this world that are as rewarding. To fly and break the bonds of the earth is indeed a heavenly feeling. So it is with becoming a leader. Often we fail to achieve our dreams, not through lack of effort, but because we aimed too low. Let the secrets and stories in this book raise your sights to a new level—to the level of a Pilot-Leader.

Taking flight and balancing in midair

The beauty of a helicopter, an incredible engineering achievement by any standard, can be summed up best by one word: hover. When every part of the helicopter is working in sync, the pilot can lift the aircraft up off the ground to a stable position over

the earth. But the key to it all lies in the cockpit. This is where a pilot must trust in the incredible forces the aircraft is producing.

This leap of faith can easily be illustrated by new pilots learning how to hover. New pilots will already know that to achieve a stable hover they must get all of the control inputs in unison. It is a time of contrasts: pilots must be firm on the controls but relaxed. They are moving the controls, but the aircraft isn't moving. Pilots are focused outside the helicopter but keenly aware of what is going on inside. They're working hard but hardly moving. In essence, pilots must become in tune with the aircraft. They must anticipate how the aircraft is going to respond to their control inputs and then not put them in unnecessarily. Pilots must think ahead two or three nonmovements. They must anticipate wind gusts but not too forcefully. They must control the aircraft but not overcontrol. During this most delicate of maneuvers, pilots must move the controls imperceptively. To do otherwise will result in wild gyrations of the airframe.

This delicate balance of hovering is actually a state of

being that scientists call homeostasis and once you achieve it as a leader, you'll experience greater success than you have ever thought possible. Homeostasis is defined as: "a state of physiological equilibrium produced by a balance of functions and of chemical composition within an organism." This state of balance is not just about getting your team in sync but about getting your being, your physiological self in balance. It is more than just getting the people on your team or in your business together for a project; it's about raising their functions to a state of equilibrium.

Soaring toward a goal

How does a pilot reach a destination? By moving straight forward toward the goal? Wrong! As a pilot or sailor will tell you, to fly "straight" requires a multitude of corrections. As external forces begin to act on you and your team, a constant "eye on the prize" and regular course corrections are necessary to bring you back on track to take you to your goals much quicker. Try to steer directly at your target and you will miss it by a mile.

Your flight plan is a plan from which you will most

certainly have to deviate. Expect it. Welcome it. Do it. As Emerson wrote over a century and a half ago: "The voyage of the best ship [and aircraft!] is a zigzag line of a hundred tacks."

We have a lot to learn from successful Pilot-Leaders. They have reached a level of achievement worthy of study and emulation but not adoration or idolatry. They are human. Somewhere along the line, though, they learned what it took to be a success. They gained the necessary knowledge and experience to propel them to the top of their field of endeavor.

Most people who attain noteworthy achievements in life pattern their success after someone that they admire, perhaps a mentor or a role model. Using a role model can be a shortcut to success. If you find someone who is achieving the type of results that you desire, then pattern your behavior after theirs and you will see results. However, I recommend taking this one step further.

As you model someone else's behavior, you must also think for yourself. Not by coincidence, this is what also separates the good pilots from the few excep-

tional pilots: their ability to "think."

Thomas J. Watson, Sr., the founder of IBM, had this one word emblazoned everywhere in his company. It soon became the company mantra and today continues to help separate IBM from the other information technology companies, making it still the largest such company in the United States.

Developing more Pilot-Leaders on your team

It is a safe bet that there are fewer companies who have established professional development programs for their employees than those that haven't. Companies continue to spend millions of dollars to search outside their own walls for good leaders. The marketplace shows us that companies would rather pay a search firm than implement an effective leadership development program.

You as a Pilot-Leader can break out of this pattern and establish your own Leadership Flight School to produce leaders just as the Army grooms the pilots of tomorrow at Fort Rucker, Alabama.

Let's look at the curriculum of an ordinary future

pilot (if there is such a thing) undergoing what the U.S. Army has dubbed, Initial Entry Rotary Wing Training or what civilians would call Helicopter Flight School (the government may produce the best pilots but they are the worst at bureaucratic names!). Here at the world's largest heliport, future pilots are taught the essentials of helicopter flight.

As these pilots learn to fly, you, too, can teach your team to lead. Remember, just as pilots are made not born, leaders are also made not born.

A quick look at the Army's Helicopter Flight Training reveals that while the classroom instruction can prepare you to strap into the cockpit, you must eventually take the controls to really *learn* how to fly. Remember *that* when your team members are learning to be leaders. As a Chinese proverb says:

> "Tell me—I'll forget.
> Show me—I might remember.
> Involve me—and I'll understand."

In pilot training, the students first read about the maneuver. They then sit and watch while the instructor pilots demonstrate the same maneuver for them.

Finally, the student takes the controls and *attempts* the maneuver. This three-step procedure works and works well. Use it when teaching your future leaders.

Notice above I said "*attempts.*" If the flight student does not perform the aerial maneuver to standard, the instructor coaches, corrects and encourages until it is perfected. This is all done to create an environment conducive to success. Provide a similar "learn by failure" environment for your future leaders and you will foster loyalty and respect in them as well.

IBM's Thomas J. Watson, Sr. put it this way: "Do you want to succeed? Then, double your rate of failure. Success lies on the far side of failure."

A note of caution: Give these fledging leaders real opportunities to earn their wings but always with a measure of caution until they are ready to go "solo." I am definitely not encouraging you to allow them to fail and potentially bring the entire team down with them. Exercise a measure of risk management and allow them to lead on small, but pivotal projects. Then step back and watch them take to the skies.

Think like a pilot

This book was designed to give you insight into the minds of pilots. The seven secrets you just explored are transferable to leadership in your chosen profession.

Make a list of the seven secrets of successful pilots and tape it to your mirror at home and put a copy somewhere at work where you will see it often during the day. Internalize these secrets and learn to think like a pilot. You will see a difference. Problems that appeared insurmountable before will be put into context. Goals that appeared out of reach will be within your grasp. As you begin to adopt the Pilot-Leader secrets as your own, you will begin to see a transformation in yourself and you will gain confidence in your abilities.

It takes repeated training flights to become a great pilot. Similarly, you will require follow-on training. This book can help. Return to these seven secrets and the questions at the end of the chapters regularly and apply your experiences. Review the Pilot-Leader secrets list daily. In addition, concentrate on your development in one of the seven areas at least once a day, and over the next seven working days, rotate the

areas so that you cover each of them. In a month you will have made progress in all seven.

This book aimed at helping you develop a new perspective on life, leadership and a whole new attitude. It's more than a positive mental attitude. Having read this book, you have the insight to think like a champion of the skies with a "*Pilot* Mental Attitude."

Einstein once remarked that the level of thinking that got us this far will not be enough to take us to the future. In essence we must think on a higher (air)plane!

A positive mental attitude is necessary, but a Pilot Mental Attitude moves you toward even higher achievement—as a Pilot-Leader with Pilot Vision!

About the Author

John Michael Magness is a professional speaker, international consultant and helicopter pilot. A Desert Storm veteran as well as a former special operations pilot, he flew with the most elite helicopter force, the fabled Nightstalkers, conducting secret missions around the world. He has an aerospace engineering degree from the U.S. Military Academy at West Point and a Masters in Business from Boston University. He lives with his wife, daughter and son in Fort Worth, Texas.

John Michael Magness conducts training seminars and motivational programs internationally. His unique "pilot" perspective and delivery have won rave reviews among professionals who also desire to fly toward higher success.

For additional information:

e-mail *pilotbook@aol.com* or
visit *http://www.pilotbook.com*

The sky is truly *not* your limit.